PUBL. DATE
OCT. 1

NOTES ON CHOPIN

ANDRÉ GIDE

NOTES

ON

CHOPIN

Translated from the French
by BERNARD FRECHTMAN

PHILOSOPHICAL LIBRARY
NEW YORK

PRINTED IN THE UNITED STATES OF AMERICA

TABLE OF CONTENTS

DEDICATION

I DEDICATE *these pages to the memory of the Reverend Father, director of Monte Cassino, who, a few years before the war, received me in that famous monastery. Here is why:*

Dom Adelberto Gresnitch, whom I had met in Rome, had very kindly invited me to go into retreat for a short time at Monte Cassino. We had several mutual friends, including Maurice Denis, who had just done his portrait. Dom Adelberto, who was of Dutch origin, spoke several languages equally well. A highly cultivated man, his con-

versation was captivating. I accepted his offer at once. The order of Saint Benoit is a hospitable order; that is, certain rooms and halls are set aside for travelers. But Dom Adelberto thought quite rightly that it would be more interesting for me to participate intimately in the monastic life. He therefore arranged for a cell to be put at my disposal and for me to take my meals, not with the tourists, but in the great refectory of the order. I expected to spend only three days at Monte Cassino; but these days were so instructive, the big cell had so fine a view and the society of the Benedictines was so charming, that I lingered with them for a whole unforgettable week.

I should, upon entering the monastery, have paid my respects to the Reverend Father, but he was ill and sent word to me that he could not receive me at once. It was not until the morning of my departure that he permitted me to ex-

II

press my gratitude to him. *This formal-
ity appeared to me to be a painful duty
which, I admit, made me quite appre-
hensive, and it was tremblingly that I
entered an enormous hall where the
Reverend Father awaited me and where
Dom Adelberto, who ushered me in, left
me.*

*The Reverend Father was extremely
aged. Of German origin, he spoke Italian and French admirably; but what was
I to say to him? He was in a big arm-
chair, which his weakness prevented
him from leaving. He bade me sit down
near him. And his kindness was such
that I quickly felt at ease. As soon as the
first greetings were done with, we began
to talk about music.*

*"I know that you love it," he said,
"and that you have been performnig
these last few evenings in the company
of Dom Adelberto and some of our
other people. I have much regretted not*

being able to be with you, for I too love music very much. I have been told that you have been able to put our mediocre piano to good use. I too played the piano. But for a long time I have had to give it up and content myself with reading without performing. Are you aware that reading music silently in this way and hearing it in imagination is a perfect joy? Yes, when I have to remain lying down, as often happens, it is not the **Church Fathers** or other books that I send for, but rather musical scores."

He paused for a few moments, anxious to see whether I was following him, then:

"And what do you think I send for? ... No, it's not Bach; it's not even Mozart ... It's Chopin." And he added: "That is the purest of music."

"The purest of music." That is quite right, something I should have hardly dared say and am anxious to shelter with

IV

DEDICATION

all the authority of so important and so aged a religious dignitary. Surprising words, but they will be understood by those for whom the music of Chopin is not (or at least is not merely) that profane and brilliant thing which performers present to us in concerts.

But the most surprising thing about those words is that they were uttered by a German; for, it seems to me, there is no music less Germanic. Had Barrès been a musician, what a Lorrainer he would have made of Chopin in the name of his early Nancy origins. Though I may recognize in Chopin's work a Polish inspiration, a Polish spring, I am also pleased to recognize in this raw cloth a French cut, a French fashion. Am I going too far? Let us suppose that there is nothing particularly French in the composition of his poems, but that rather continuous association with the French spirit, with French cul-

ture, led him to exaggerate the qualities of the Slavic genius that were precisely the most anti-Germanic.

In like manner, the composer I wish to contrast with Wagner is not Bizet, as Nietzsche was fond of doing, and not without spite, but Chopin. And if objection is made that there is a ridiculous disproportion with the enormous mass of Wagner, and that in comparison with his gigantic work the work of Chopin seems incomparably slight, I shall answer that it is precisely in that respect that I first wish to contrast them and that it is because of its enormousness that Wagner's work seems to me most Germanic. I feel this enormousness not only in the inhuman length of each work, but in excesses of all kinds, in the insistence, in the number of instruments, in the overworking of the voices, in the pathos. Before him, music had become particularly effusive, displaying

VI

DEDICATION

*emotions as amply and intensely as it
could. Chopin, on the other hand, was
the first to banish all oratorical development. His sole concern, it seems, is to
narrow limits, to reduce the means of
expression to what is indispensable. Far
from charging his emotion with notes,
in the manner of Wagner, for example,
he charges each note with emotion, and
I was about to say: with responsibility.
And though there are doubtless greater
musicians, there is none more perfect.
With the result that the work of Chopin,
hardly more voluminous in its kind than
the poetic work of Baudelaire, is comparable to* **Les Fleurs du Mal** *in the intense concentration and significance of
the best pieces that compose it, and
through the extraordinary influence that
both of them, for that very reason, were
able to exert.*

NOTES ON CHOPIN

I ANNOUNCED my "Notes on Chopin" as early as 1892, almost forty years ago. It is true that at the time I announced: "Notes on Schumann and Chopin." Today the coupling of these names causes me a malaise comparable to that which Nietzsche said he experienced before "Goethe *and* Schiller." At the time, it seemed to me that there was much to be said about Schumann too; but it has seemed to me less and less important.

Schumann is a poet. Chopin is an *artist,* which is quite different; I shall go into this later on.

But, by a strange destiny peculiar to him, the more the performers of Chopin try to spread a knowledge of his work, the more he is misunderstood, Bach, Scarlatti, Beethoven, Schumann, Liszt or Fauré can be more or less well interpreted. One does not falsify their meaning by slightly distorting their character. Chopin is the only one who is betrayed, who can be deeply, intimately, totally violated.

Have you ever heard actors declaiming Baudelaire as if they were doing Casimir Delavigne? They play Chopin as if it were Liszt. They do not understand the difference. Thus presented, better Liszt. There the virtuoso finds at least something to take hold of, something to be taken with; through him, Liszt truly allows himself to be grasped.

NOTES ON CHOPIN

Chopin utterly escapes him, and so subtly that, indeed, the public does not suspect it.

We are told that when he was at the piano Chopin always looked as if he were improvising; that is, he seemed to be constantly seeking, inventing, discovering his thought little by little. This kind of charming hesitation, of surprise and delight, ceases to be possible if the work is presented to us, no longer in a state of successive formation, but as an already perfect, precise and objective whole. I see no other meaning in the titles that he was fond of giving to certain of his most exquisite pieces: *Impromptus*. I do not think it possible to admit that Chopin improvised them, in the strict sense of the term. No. But it is essential to play them in such a way that they seem to be improvised, that is, with a certain, I dare not say slowness, but uncertainty; in any case, without that

21

unbearable assurance which a headlong movement carries with it. It is a promenade of discoveries, and the performer should be cautious about giving the impression of knowing in advance what he is going to say, or that all of it is already written down; I like the musical phrase which gradually shapes beneath his fingers to seem to be emerging from him, to astonish even him, and subtly to invite us to enter into his delight. Even in such a work *di bravura* as the energetic and tempestuous *Etude in A minor* (the second of the Second Book), what emotion do you expect me to experience if you experience none yourself and do not let me feel that you experience any, you, a pianist, suddenly entering *A flat major,* then immediately *E major*—a sudden sunbeam piercing the torment and the shower—if you give me to understand by your assurance that you knew it in advance and that everything was prepared?

Each modulation in Chopin, never trivial and foreseen, must respect, must preserve that freshness, that emotion which almost fears the surging up of the new, that secret of wonderment to which the adventurous soul exposes itself along paths not blazed in advance, where the landscape reveals itself only gradually.

That is also why, almost always, I like the music of Chopin to be spoken in an undertone, almost in a murmur, without any brilliance (I except, obviously,

certain dashing pieces, including most
of the *scherzos* and *polonaises*), without
that unbearable assurance of the virtuoso which thus strips it of its most win-
ning allure. That is how Chopin himself played, so we are told by those who
could still hear him. He always seemed
to fall short of the fullest sonority; I
mean: almost never made the piano
yield its full sound, and thereby very
often disappointed his audience which
thought that it "hadn't gotten its
money's worth."

Chopin proposes, supposes, insinu-
ates, seduces, persuades; he almost never
asserts.

And the more reticent his thought
becomes, the better do we listen to it. I
have in mind that "confessional tone"
which Laforgue praised in Baudelaire.

Someone knowing Chopin only
through the too clever virtuosi might
take him for a purveyor of show-pieces

... whom I would detest, were I not able to question him myself, were he not able to say to me in a low voice: "Don't listen to them. Through them, there is nothing more you can say. And I suffer much more than you from what they have made of me. Better to be ignored than taken for what I am not."

The swooning of certain listeners before certain famous interpreters of Chopin irritates me. What is there to like in them? All that is left is the worldly and the profane. Nothing that, like the song of Rimbaud's bird, "stops you and makes you blush."

I HAVE often heard Beethoven compared to Michael Angelo, Mozart to Correggio, to Giorgione, etc. Although these comparisons between artists of different arts seem to me rather futile, I can not refrain from observing how often remarks which I might make about Chopin are equally applicable to Baudelaire, and vice versa. So that, in speaking of Chopin, the name of Baudelaire has come quite naturally to my pen a number of times. Chopin's works used to be called "unhealthy music." *Les Fleurs du Mal* used to be called "unhealthy poetry," and, I rather think, for the same reasons. Both have a like concern for perfection, an equal horror of rhetoric, declamation and oratorical development; but I would like particularly to note that I find in both the same use of *surprise* and of the extraordinary foreshortenings which achieve it.

When, at the beginning of the *Ballade in G minor* and immediately after the opening, in order to introduce the major theme which he later takes up in different keys and with new sonorities, after a few indecisive measures in *F* where only the tonic and the fifth are given, Chopin unexpectedly sounds a deep *B flat* which suddenly alters the landscape like the stroke of an enchanter's wand, this incantatory boldness seems to me comparable to a surprising

28

foreshortening by the poet of *Les Fleurs du Mal.*

Moreover, it seems to me that, in the history of music, Chopin occupies, approximately, the place (and plays the role) of Baudelaire in the history of

poetry, both of them having been misunderstood at first, and for similar reasons.

Ah! how hard it is to struggle against a false image! In addition to the Chopin of the virtuosi, there is the Chopin of young ladies. A too sentimental Chopin.

29

He *was* that, alas! but he was not only
that. Yes, to be sure, there is the melancholy Chopin who even drew from the
piano the most heart-broken sobs. But,
to hear certain people talk, it seems that
he never left the minor. What I love and
what I praise him for is that through
and beyond this sadness he nevertheless
attains joy; it is because the joy in him
is dominant (Nietzsche felt this very
well); a joy which has nothing of the
somewhat hasty and vulgar gaiety of
Schumann; a felicity which joins hands
with that of Mozart, but more human,
participating in nature, and also incor-
porated in the landscape that may be
found in the ineffable smile of the scene
at the water's edge in Beethoven's *Pas-
torale*. Before Debussy and certain Rus-
sians, I do not think that music was ever
so shot through with the play of light,
with the murmur of water, with wind
and foliage. *Sfogato,* he wrote; has any

other musician ever used this word, would he have ever had the desire, the need, to indicate the airing, the breath of breeze, which, interrupting the rhythm, contrary to all hope, comes freshening and perfuming the middle of his barcarolle?

How simple are Chopin's musical propositions! Nothing comparable here to what any other musician had done before him; the latter (I exclude Bach, however) start with an emotion, like a poet who then seeks words to express it. In the manner of Valéry, who, quite the contrary, starts with the word, with the verse, Chopin, like a perfect artist, starts with notes (this too is what made people say that he "improvised"); but, more than Valéry, he at once allows a quite human emotion to invade this very sim-

31

ple situation, which he enlarges so that it becomes magnificent.

Yes, Chopin, and it is very important that this be noted, lets himself be led and counseled by the notes; one might say that he meditates upon the expressive power of each one. He feels that a certain note or a certain double note, a third or a sixth, changes meaning depending upon its position in the scale and, through an unexpected modification of the bass, suddenly makes it say something other than what it said at first. Therein lies his expressive power.

I admit that I do not understand the title that Chopin liked to give to those short *pieces:* Preludes. Preludes to what? Each of Bach's preludes is followed by its fugue; it is an integral part of it. But I find it hardly easier to imagine any one of these preludes of Chopin followed by any other piece in the same key, be it by the same author, than all of these preludes of Chopin played immediately one after the other. Each one of them is a prelude to a meditation; nothing can be less a concert piece; nowhere has Chopin revealed himself more intimately. Each of them, or almost (and some of them are extremely short), creates a particular atmosphere, establishes an emotional setting, then *fades out as a bird alights. All is still.*

Not all are of equal importance. Some are charming, others terrifying. None are indifferent.

The first *Prelude* is, among all of Chopin's compositions, one of those which most readily give rise to misunderstanding, one of those which can

most easily be spoiled, whose misinterpretation seems to me most monstrous.
Taking as authority the word *agitato* in-
scribed at the head of the selection, all
performers, without exception (at least
to my knowledge), here launch forth in
a frenzied, reckless movement. Is it
likely, I ask you, that at the threshold of
this book, in the most limpid of tones,
Chopin desired so disturbing a manifes-
tation? Think of the first *Etude,* likewise in *C major,* so serene. Think of the
two *Preludes in C major* of the *Well-
tempered Clavichord;* what purity, what
calm; what a quiet and evident proposition. Think of Bach's organ preludes in
the same key; of their extraordinary *introductory* character. And I am by no
means trying to liken this *Prelude* of
Chopin to those of Bach. But I rather
like to see there, at the head of the book,
a kind of very simple ornamental front,
one that invites. Like the first prelude of

Bach's *Clavichord,* it offers at the start a very pure phrase, which develops fully only after taking a new breath. A first impulsion forms a perfect unit, of four measures in Bach, of eight measures in Chopin, and returns to the starting-point; then takes off anew for a more complete prize whose possibility was merely indicated by the first departure. To manage to make of this exquisite offering something chaotic is a *tour de force* which the virtuoso achieves and which leaves me dumbfounded. This piece, quite the contrary, should be played very casually; no strife should be felt in it, no effort. It is fitting that the discreet melody be not abandoned only to the upper part of the last two fingers of the hand, which merely double at the octave the melody of the middle part which Chopin was careful to indicate "tenuto"; an indication which, quite often, is not observed, and which nevertheless is of the utmost importance. Yes, this work, in its entirety, is simply like a lovely, quiet wave (despite the *agitato*

which usually is pushed to the point of tempest), preceded by another and smaller wave, and the whole draws to a close in an eddying which dies out gently.

In general, for Chopin's music, but why not say it here and now, since nowhere is it more applicable than in this short piece, the performer "adopts" too rapid a movement (half again too rapid here). Why? Perhaps because Chopin's music is not in itself difficult enough and the pianist is bent on showing off, as if it were much more difficult, when one attains a certain mastery, to play quickly than to play slowly. Above all through tradition. The performer who, indeed, for the first time, would *dare* (for a certain courage is needed) to play Chopin's music in the proper *tempo,* that is, *much more slowly than is customary,* would really be bringing out its meaning for the first time, and in a way capable of plunging his audience into a deep ecstasy: which is Chopin's due. The way he is usually played, the way all the virtuosi play him, hardly anything remains but the *effect.* All the rest is imperceptible, which, indeed, signifies above all: the very secret of a work in which no note is negligible, in which no rhetoric enters, no redundancy, where nothing is simple padding, as happens so often in the music of so many other composers, and I speak even of the greatest.

The cinema has enabled us to see the surprising grace which a human or animal gesture can achieve when it is shown in slow-motion; imperceptible when the movement is rapid. It is not a question here (though one may do it) of slowing down the *tempo* of Chopin's music excessively. It is very simply a matter of not hurrying it, of allowing it its natural movement, easy as breathing. I should like to inscribe, at the head of Chopin's work, the exquisite verses of Valéry:

> *Est-il art plus tendre*
> *Que cette lenteur?* . . .
> (Is there art more gentle
> Than this slowness?)

And it goes without saying that a number of Chopin's pieces (the *scherzos* in particular and the finales of the sonatas) involve a fantastically rapid pace, but, in general, each virtuoso indiscriminately plays almost all of Chopin's compositions *as quickly as possible,* and that is what I find monstrous. At any rate, the verses of Valéry nowhere find a more striking application than in the first *Prelude.*

A few words more about this first *Prelude:* the melody, in a manner of which we shall find a few other examples in Chopin's work, is found obstinately reflected in the higher octave, so subtly and plausibly that it permits the sensitive performer to accentuate the first indication or its reflection as he pleases, thus broadening the phrase.

In addition, this first indication never falls exactly on the strong beat marked by the bass, but rather immediately after it, which gives to the melody a charmingly indecisive kind of spiritedness. It would be a serious mistake to give a systematically greater importance and accent to one or the other of these two voices which sing after one another in unison. Sometimes one prevails, sometimes the other; at times they almost blend. Often there are, strictly speaking, no voices in *Chopin;* he did not write for singing but, to be exact, for

the piano, and it often happens (in certain *Nocturnes*—the Seventh, Eighth and Ninth, for example—in particular)

that in the course of a selection he intro-
duces a second brief voice, as if for an
uncertain duo, which is soon inter-
rupted and reabsorbed into the whole.
The piece would appear ill composed if
the pianist, anxious to give too much
emphasis to the melody, were to evoke
two instruments, a violin and a viola,
one of which would thenceforth remain
idle almost constantly.

Unbearable practise of certain pianists, *phrasing* Chopin and punctuating,
so to speak, the melody. Whereas the
fact is that what is most exquisite and
most individual in Chopin's art, where-
in it differs most wonderfully from all
others, I see in just that non-interrup-
tion of the phrase; the insensible, the
imperceptible gliding from one melodic
proposition to another, which leaves or
gives to a number of his compositions
the fluid appearance of streams.

Whereby this music recalls the non-discontinuous melody of the Arabian clarinet which never allows us to feel the moment when the musician takes a fresh breath. There are no longer any periods or commas; and that is why I can not approve the "organ points" which certain ill-advised editors and performers have added in the Chorale of the *Nocturne in G minor,* for the satisfaction of fools. . . .

It is particularly interesting to know that the two *Preludes,* in *D minor* and *A minor,* were composed a good while before the others. They are by far the strangest, the most bewildering of the whole collection. It is quite understandable that they astonished Chopin's contemporaries, particularly the one in *A minor.* First considered, it seems, as a simple musical oddity by no means lend-

42

ing itself to performance. "Is not this an ugly, wretched, hopeless, almost grotesque and discordant *Prelude?*" said Huneker, who kept attributing the supposed imperfections of this very short piece to Chopin's sickly condition.

It is, to be sure, the most discordant of all, and dissonance can not be pushed further. It really seems as if Chopin were tending to go to his very limits, to regions where the inner being is out of tune. And what makes the disharmony of this selection more striking is that it appears quite inevitable and to flow necessarily from what is given at the beginning. It seems that, here as often, Chopin has set himself a problem: what would happen if . . . ? The upper part (let us call it, to please some, the melody), very simple, very calm, has nothing in itself which could not conclude in peace, in harmony; but the lower one pursues its inevitable march, uncon-

cerned with the human plaint. And
from this discord, let us call it, if you
like, between man and fatality, is born
an anguish which, to my knowledge,
music has never, before or since, expressed better. This fatal lower part is
itself composed of two voices, which it is
important that the performer keep very
distinct; one encroaching upon the
other, by means of a great distance of a

tenth and an eleventh, the other constantly hesitating, often as if groping between the major and the minor.

I must admit that, despite all my admiration for Chopin, it took me a long

44

time to appreciate this piece. It appeared to me particularly odd, and I had difficulty seeing how a performer could turn it to good account. The reason is, and I understand it today, that there is no *account* for it to be turned to. I am of the opinion that it must be played without any striving for *effect,* very simply, but with an implacable and perfect clarity. And in the most discordant part —I mean from the tenth to the fifteenth measure—one should not seek to diminish the effect of the discord, whether by the pedal or by a timid *pianissimo.* And if—I mean during these few measures— it is fatality which triumphs, the voice which at first sang now no longer even tries to make itself understood. When it continues a little later on, it is solitary and, as it were, weary. Not only may the part for the left hand not be, ought not be, considered as an accompaniment, but, quite the contrary, it seems as if the upper and lower parts are at grips with one another. And when, at the very end of the piece, a certain resigned serenity seems possible, it is because the fatal lower part, after a brief re-entry, has definitely withdrawn.

Oh! no, indeed, this is not a concert piece. I can not see any audience liking it. But played in a whisper for oneself alone, its indefinable emotion can not be exhausted, nor that kind of almost physical terror, as if one were before a world glimpsed in passing, of a world hostile to tenderness, from which human affection is excluded.

In the *Prelude in D Minor,* the last of the collection, there likewise breathes this inexorable fatality. Dizzily remote notes are bound together by immense leaps. Here, in the melodic part too, no gentleness, but a reflection of that inexorability which the brutal bass accentuates hideously, so to speak. The mid-

46

dle part of the arpeggiated chord of the bass (the dominant most of the time, and particularly in the first nine meas-

ures) is indicated as being held at first, that is, marked as both a sixteenth note and as a quarter. This quarter ceases to be marked from the tenth measure on. I should like to know whether this indication at the beginning (then the discontinuance of indication) is Chopin's. It seems to me interesting to repeat it in various places, that is, to consider this second note as being held. Certain editions indicate the upper note of the lower part, the fifth of each group,

47

as staccato or at least legato. It may be.
Ah! when shall we have a correct edition
of Chopin revised in accordance with
the manuscripts? The few times I have
had occasion to hear this *Prelude* performed—too rapidly, as always, the per-
sistently repeated group of the five lower
notes reduced to a confused buzzing . . .
—the performer seemed to fear monotony, to be terrified by that kind of de-
liberate ugliness which, quite the contrary, has merely to be accentuated, by
implacably marking, through the rhythm of this group of five notes, another
rhythm, again implacable, marked by
the note of the extreme bass (the tonic
most often), which returns with a perfectly regular hammering, *cutting this
six-beat measure into four parts,* that is,
creating a second rhythm absolutely in-
dependent of the first.

I have elsewhere strongly protested
against that reputation for nostalgic

melancholy which is given, usually without discrimination, to all of Chopin's
music, in which I have so many times
encountered the expression of the high-
est joy. But really, in these two preludes
I find only the most sombre despair. Yes,
despair; the word "melancholy" is no
longer pertinent here; a feeling of the
inexorable, twice cut through, in the
last measures of the *Prelude in D minor,*
by a harrowing moan,

spasmodically taken up a second time in
a twisted, jolted and, as it were, sobbing
rhythm; then swept by the implacable
final run, which concludes *fortissimo* in

frightful depths where one touches the floor of Hell.

The *Prelude in F sharp minor* has an air of *perpetuum mobile,* like so many other compositions of Chopin. No pause, from one end of the work to the other; but nonetheless, here the phrases are quite distinct, though closely bound together. However rapid the movement of this *Prelude* may be, I like to begin it with a bit of uncertainty, indictating the theme very clearly and distinctly, allowing the listener to wait with some curiosity for what Chopin will do with it. The first phrase, as often in Chopin's music, is repeated with a different conclusion. Yes indeed, perfectly composed as this work may be, I like to let it keep the appearanec of an impromptu; I mean: the impression of a successive discovery, of an advance into the unknown. The groups of thirty-second notes, though indicated in small letters, should not be played *pianissimo* and like simple grace-notes. I like to give them an intensity of sound almost equal to that of the notes held by the thumb; it is quite enough for this note to be held in order to give it the preponderance which is due it, because it serves as a basis for all the others. I should like this

dense group of six notes (always followed by a note repeated in the octave)
to be considered as a single block, each
one coupled with the following one.
These little notes, emanating, so to
speak, from the first, in the manner of
harmonics, molding the sonority, and
precisely defining the constantly moving
tonality, are an integral part of the fundamental note. If the latter appears too

distinct, nothing remains but a brilliant
piece, a facile melody, and the whole
gravity, the very meaning of the piece is
lost. On the other hand, by giving an
almost equal intensity of sound to all
the notes, this prelude once again be-

comes admirable, one of the loveliest compositions in the collection.

If I complain that most of Chopin's pieces are played much too quickly, I must say that, on the other hand, the *Prelude in B minor* seems to me to be often played too slowly. It seems that an effort is made to make it melancholy, as melancholy as possible . . . I remember having heard it performed in accompaniment to a recitation of a poem of Baudelaire. Thus, the music and the poetry were equally compromised. Let us leave this invention to those who really like neither one nor the other.

Without exactly speaking about imitative music, the obstinate repetition of the higher note (the tonic) in this *Prelude in B minor* and of the dominant in the *Prelude in D flat* should be loud and distinct, indifferent to the melody which crosses it, monotonous, implacable, like a persistent rain-drop, like an elemental force indifferent to human emotion, consequently without any preciosity or affectation.

I feel no need, in order to enjoy music, to see it in terms of literature or painting, and am very little preoccupied with the "meaning" of a work. It narrows it and cramps me. And that is also why, despite the amazing blendings of Schubert, Schumann or Fauré, I am especially pleased by music without words or, at the very most, the kind for which the *mystique* of a liturgy is a pretext. Music escapes the material world and enables us to escape it. Yet, though certain preludes *(in G major and F major)* may not evoke any precise landscape (for me, at least), I irresistibly liken the murmur of the lower part of one and the upper part of the other to the discrete purling of a stream. In both, the few singing notes, which reduce to its simplest form what one no longer dares call a melody, seem dictated and motivated by this murmur, as if emanating from it spontaneously. And even, in the *Prelude in G,* these notes are simply the very same ones, though more spaced, offered by that untrustworthy accompaniment in a subtle and discrete invitation.

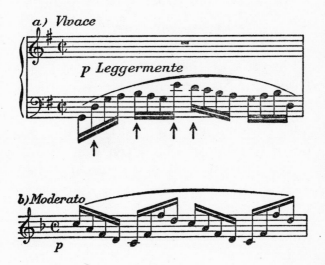

It is well to note it and to make it felt almost imperceptibly; which can not be
done when this prelude is played, as by
most virtuosi, with intolerable haste.
What ease, what serenity! In both,
hardly do we leave the initial key for a
moment for one nearby than we rejoin
the key of the beginning. Chopin here
renounces all subtlety, those mysterious
vague keys into which he was later to
drive all modern music, after having so
greatly surprised and at times irritated
the ears of his contemporaries. And it
astonishes me that, denying himself all
ruses and his most individual artifices,
he still remains so personal that one can
not imagine these few utterly simple and
polished measures being written by another, and that he is never more Chopin
than when he seems least to try to be.
No rhetorical development, no desire to
inflate the musical idea and get more out
of it, but rather to simplify his expres-

sion to the extreme, to the point of perfection.

FRAGMENTS FROM THE JOURNAL

We have thought it useful to follow the Notes on Chopin *with* Fragments from the Journal *and* Unpublished Pages *which relate to Chopin and, more generally, to music.*

September 1893.

MOZART'S joy: a joy one feels to be lasting; Schumann's joy is feverish, one feels it coming between two sobs. Mozart's joy is made up of serenity; and the phrase of his music is like a tranquil thought; his simplicity is merely purity; it is a crystalline thing; there all emotions frolic, but as if already celestially transposed. "Moderation consists in feeling emotion as the angels do!" (Joubert). One must think of Mozart to understand what that really means.

FRAGMENTS FROM JOURNAL

Naples, January 29, 1896.

This landscape demands its own music, open like itself, bright with laughter born without laborious gestation.

I am amazed to find here in Naples that very strange Oriental song, begun on too shrill a note, which rushes oddly down to the tonic in two parallel phrases, turned as if between two keys, spasmodically stressed and then abruptly stifled.

FRAGMENTS FROM JOURNAL

Biskra, April 1896.

"Who invented music?" asks Athman. I answer, "Musicians." He isn't satisfied; he insists. I answer gravely that God did. "No," he replies immediately, "it was the devil."

And he explains to me that to the Arabs all musical instruments are instruments of Hell, except the two-stringed viol, whose name I couldn't remember, with a very long neck and a sound-box made of a hollowed tortoise. Street-singers, poets, prophets and story-tellers play it, with a small bow, and accompany themselves, and sometimes so sweetly that, says Athman, "a gate of heaven seems to open."

May 22, 1907.

Last night, Strauss' *Salomé* . . .

Execrable romantic music, with an orchestral rhetoric enough to make you like Bellini. Only the parts that are comically (the magi) or morbidly picturesque, Salomé's reticence when Herod wants to make her dance—almost the entire role of Herod, reveal a remarkable competence. Lasserre notes likewise the excellence of the comic truculence in Hugo;—likewise *Die Meistersinger—same causes.* And same causes for the defects: indiscretion of means and monotony of effects, tedious insistence, flagrant insincerity; never-ending mobilization of all resources. Same for Hugo as for Wagner, when metaphors pour into his head to express an idea, he won't choose, won't spare us a single one. Fundamental lack of artistry in this.

FRAGMENTS FROM JOURNAL

January 25, 1908.

Inquiry of the *Berliner Tageblatt*.

It concerns questioning, on the occasion of the twenty-fifth anniversary of Wagner's death, "the artistic and intellectual luminaries of all Europe as to their opinion on the influence of Wagnerism, especially in France."

I answer:

"I abhor the person and the work of Wagner; my passionate aversion has only increased since my childhood. This prodigious genius does not exalt so much as he *crushes*. He has enabled a host of snobs, literary people and fools to think that they like music, and a few artists to think that genius can be learned. Germany has perhaps never produced anything at once so great and so barbaric."

FRAGMENTS FROM JOURNAL

When E flat made its entrée into the drawing-room, C and G considered it a third person.

"It's a dominant," thought A flat, while E natural cried out, "I recognize it: it's my leading tone."

. . . But the same holds here as in music where the chord of G sharp has not the same meaning, depending on whether you reach it by way of the sharps or of the flats, and does not sound the same as that of A flat to the sensitive ear, though composed of the same notes.

May 14, 1921.

. . . I hate virtuosity, but it always inspires me with respect and I would like, in order to despise it with conviction, to be first of all capable of it; I would like to be sure that I were not the fox in the fable; I *know* and *feel,* for example, that Chopin's Barcarolle *should* be played much more slowly than Mlle. X does, . . . than they all do;—but in order to play it before others as *leisurely* as I like, I should have to know that I could just as well play it much more quickly, and above all feel that the listener is convinced of this. Played at this rate, Chopin's music becomes *brilliant,* loses its characteristic value, its virtue . . .

FRAGMENTS FROM JOURNAL

June 3, 1921.

. . . Returned to Chopin's *Barcarolle* which is not so difficult to play more quickly as I had thought; and I'm getting there (I let myself be far too intimidated by the *brio* of others),—but in this way it loses all character, all emotion, all *languor;* and *that above all* is what is expressed in this admirable work: the languor in excessive joy. It seems that there is too much sound, too many notes once one no longer understands the perfect significance of each one. Any good performance should be an *explanation* of the work. But the pianist strives for *effect,* like the actor; and effect is usually obtained only at the expense of the text. The performer knows very well that the less I understand, the more amazed I shall be. But the fact is that what I want is to understand. Astonishment in art has value only if it yields immediately to emotion; and most often it prevents it.

FRAGMENTS FROM JOURNAL

December 1, 1921.

I have gone back to the piano; am amazed that I now play Beethoven's *Sonatas* so easily—at least those over which I worked a great deal in the past and then put aside. But their pathos exhausts me, and what satisfies me most today is Bach, and perhaps above all his *Art of the Fugue* of which I can not tire. Hardly anything human is left, and it is no longer feeling or passion which it awakens but adoration. What calm! What acceptance of all that is superior to man! What disdain of the flesh! What peace!

December 7, 1921.

Every evening I plunge for half an
hour into the *Art of the Fugue*. Nothing that I said about it the other day now
seems to me to be quite exact. No, often
one no longer feels in it either serenity
or beauty; but rather torment of spirit
and a will to bend forms, rigid as laws
and inhumanly inflexible. It is the triumph of mind over numeral; and, before the triumph, the struggle. And,
though yielding to constraint, through
it, in spite of it, or *thanks to it,* all possible play, emotion, tenderness, and, all
things considered, harmony.

FRAGMENTS FROM JOURNAL

October 30, 1927.

Don't ask me how we went, by what
sudden leap or what unforeseen modulation, from the country of F sharp into
that of F natural. All at once it seemed
to us as if all nature were turning human, were losing, along with its excessive brilliance, that kind of vibrant tart-
ness of the greenery that both delighted
us and separated us from it. F natural, I
repeated to myself; and nothing could
be more natural than this key of F! The
landscape grew moderate. It was good to
live there. I was already acclimatizing
my thought to it; I meditated upon it, I
loved there at my ease, when suddenly,
undeniably, E flat, as with the wave of a
magic wand, like an abrupt ray falling
through a rift in the sky, like the unexpected return of a friend, came all at
once to incline our joy gently toward

more tenderness and piety. We were entering B flat.

How charming Alibert was yesterday
when he cried out, "I'd give all of Beethoven's symphonies, yes, you heard me,
all the symphonies, for a single *Ballade*
of Chopin."

FRAGMENTS FROM JOURNAL

February 28, 1928.

There is a certain relationship between the third and the fifth which is found from one octave to the next, giving by inversion the sixth, the whole forming the perfect chord. Yes, from octave to octave the number of vibrations (a number I do not know) must be in a constant relationship. And this in all keys.

And I would doubtless find them, with infinitely higher vibration figures, in the visual domain, in the perception of colors. The ear and eye allow an immediate intuition of these relationships. And it surprises me that both of our senses, as a result of gradual familiarity, a kind of domesticating, reach the point of enjoying other relationships, whose effect, at first, they consider as disagreeable to the ear and eye, as *dissonant*. (Perhaps, or probably, those which do not have a "common factor" among them.)

Yes, the interval of the minor seventh and, consequently, that of the major second, of which it is the inversion, must at the very beginning and for a long time thereafter have seemed painful to the ear, something to be avoided. Then it became pleasurable, as did the augmented fourth, both of these intervals allowing transition from one key to another, modulation, which very soon became a delight to the ear.

In our time these too simple, too familiar relationships have no further charm for our jaded ears. The ear accepts augmented and diminished intervals which at first were painful to it. The major seventh is no more proscribed than the minor second. And it goes without saying that the ear acquires a taste for these dissonances, just as, in another domain, the eye does for subtler pictorial disharmonies.

I can not think that our senses have

grown sharper; but perhaps they are more capable of enjoying any numerical relationship whatever.

No longer aiming at consonance and harmony, where is music going? Toward a kind of barbarity. Sound itself, so slowly and exquisitely disengaged from noise, is going back to it. At first, only lords, titled people, are allowed to appear on the stage; then, the bourgeoisie, then, the plebs. When the stage has been invaded, there is very soon nothing to distinguish it from the street. But what is to be done about it? What madness to try to oppose this inevitable march! In modern music the consonant intervals of former times produce upon us the effect of something "old fogeyish."

November 5, 1928.

Eiffel Tower Radio Station. An unknown (to me) virtuoso comes along and butchers Chopin's seventeenth *Prelude*. Can it be that some people take delight in this? All that I can see is an almost hideous vulgarity, affectation, and stupid sentimentalism. Why regularly hasten the movement in the middle of each measure? Don't they see that this false agitation drives out all the charming mystery of the work? Why not let the melody emerge and disengage itself from the accompaniment; why reduce these notes, which are companions to the melody, to the rank of supernumeraries and thus make it stand out by extinguishing all the fires about it, as if for fear that the imbecilic audience may not discern it? I detest this star-melody and feel it as contrary as can be to Chopin's aesthetics. With the exception of some *cantabili* in the manner of Bellini, I hold that from the top of the key-board to the bottom, everything should be perfectly homogeneous, so that the melodic part may remain deeply involved in the friendly atmosphere created by the other voices, which evoke an immaterial, constantly shimmering landscape.

November 15, 1928.

I have been going over Bach's *Inventions* for two and three voices, (in the Busoni edition). What force, what uniform mastery even in the pages which are seemingly the slightest, and how little harm this kind of musical logic (which the method of counterpoint requires of him) does to the assertion of his thought! . . .

77

February 12, 1829.

Montesquieu, in his observations on natural history, was disturbed about the formation of the moss and mistletoe which he gathered from tree-trunks. He refused to believe with the "moderns" that both of these growths might have sprung from seeds, as the new theories had it. And whether these theories were right and Montesquieu wrong is not what troubles me here. But, taking up Montesquieu's descriptions and the observations on which he takes his stand, however false the theories they inspire in him, I am amazed how applicable certain of his phrases are if I use them metaphorically to explain the way certain musical phrases of Chopin come into being.

Montesquieu speaks of a slow thickening of the sap, which progressively coagulates, becomes opaque and very naturally turns into a stem, from which new leaves emerge.

This is exactly the way the melody should take shape, for example, in Chopin's seventeenth *Prelude*. Here no tenor enters upon the scene. The singing voice is, at the beginning, barely distinguishable; it remains deeply involved, as if drifting in the regular flow

of the six eighth-notes, where beats an impersonal heart. It happens more often than the performer, the better to stress his own emotion, thinks it necessary to give fever to that quiet pulse, which, on the contrary, I like perfectly regular.

I like the melody to take wing in a quite natural way, as if one had been expecting it to bloom; at least at the beginning of the work, for once it has spread out, the melody bursts forth and definitely takes the upper hand, to vanish away and be once again reabsorbed only toward the end. I like it to seem once again to melt into the atmosphere

> *et la voix qui chantait*
S'éteint comme un oiseau se pose.
Tout se tait.

> (and the voice that sang
Dies away as a bird alights. All is silent.)

Indeed, in this prelude, on two occasions, in the two modulations into sharp keys, Chopin attains the height of joy. And I am glad to cite these modulations, among so many others, as examples of that intense state in which joy is quite close to tears. "O heart grieved with joy," said Musset's Lorenzaccio.

There are, in Chopin's work, many passages more powerful, there are none in which joy takes on a more tender, more confident and purer accent. All is lost if, in this modulation into E major, the accent becomes triumphant. I want there an uncertain delight, full of astonishment, of surprise. Still more mysterious in the re-entry in F sharp major which follows immediately the one in E. The heart can not bear so much joy; it yields, and once the supreme note has been achieved, the B, as if attained beyond all hope, the joy subsides. This B itself has nothing triumphal about it, and after the crescendo of the lower

part, should be rendered only with a
fading force.

October 30, 1929.

Records of C.: Chopin's *Preludes*.

Sensuality absent; instead, grace and
sentimentality.

Consternation. I defy anyone not already familiar with the exquisite heart
of these preludes to discover any of it in
this performance (with a few excep-
tions).

FRAGMENTS FROM JOURNAL

November 18, 1929.

Excellent work at the piano. Ah! if only I had been better advised, guided, supported, forced, in my youth! If the pleasure I take in this study could be less self-centered! I have at times been able to play the *Preludes* (particularly those in F sharp minor and E flat major) in a manner to satisfy myself and surprise and delight someone who might have heard me. But had he been there and had I known he could hear me, my playing would have immediately turned cold.

There is a certain envelopment by the musical phrase, a certain taking possession of the listener, a certain "let-yourself-be-led" which I have never seen achieved, or even sought, by any pianist. They are satisfied with presenting the selection; their playing neither explains it nor develops it nor allows it to be discovered. I dictated a few pages about this matter yesterday, which, when I re-read them, seemed to me good. But I would like to say a good deal more about it—to speak in particular about that false grace, that affectation (delay of the upper note which has been unexpectedly flatted—in order for expectation to be deceived, it must first be built up, be made to wait—toward the end of the prelude in F major) which infallibly shows the tip of its camouflaged ear, there where true sensuality—rich, disturbing, indecent—is wanting.

Ah! how sure of itself the simpering grace of this pearly E flat seems to be, conscious of the effect it is going to create! (The Countess de Noailles entering a drawing-room. At last! It is She!)

FRAGMENTS FROM JOURNAL

I feel—and to spare—that this note is tender; do I need you to yell it at me! So let its strangeness bewilder me all by itself; don't lend a helping hand. If you do it's because you take me for a fool; and if I'm not one, then you are. I find this subtle slowness likewise intolerable in the theatre when the actor pauses briefly to allow the audience's admiration (and its applause) to take form. If I insist, it is because I take this E flat as an example of what I am going to find, scattered here and there, constantly.

FRAGMENTS FROM JOURNAL

June 9, 1930.

Have been going over, the last few days, some of Chopin's *Etudes* which I have not bothered with for a long time (the two in A flat in particular, the tenth of the first book and the first of the second), because, probably quite wrongly, they seemed to me not to offer much of a challenge and, besides, their charm seemed rather trivial. Highly amazed at what Jachimecki says of the first of these, and Hans von Bulow whom he quotes: "Anyone performing this *étude* in a really perfect way may flatter himself on having attained the loftiest summit of the Parnassus of the art of the piano, for it is perhaps the most difficult of the whole collection." Etc.—Cunning difficulty, which one can triumph over only after having well grasped it. Also worked a great deal, in order to do a good job of it, on the one in F major (the third of the second book), so exquisite in its mysterious simplicity, and so important for obtaining that special suppleness and delicacy of the wrist, required by Chopin's technique, unsuspected by Bach and even by Beethoven or Mozart. This music of Chopin appeals to qualities so special and so contrary to those required of the performer of the works of Bach that, upon then going over the Great Fugue in B minor for organ (from memory, for I don't have the Liszt score here; but I am delighted that I still remember it perfectly), I had some difficulty playing it well and it seemed to me that I was back where I used to be. With the result that this morning I leave Chopin to go back to *The Well-tempered Clavichord;* with some difficulty and, consequently, great profit.

FRAGMENTS FROM JOURNAL

June 21, 1930.

I am managing to eliminate the crescendos from my playing (at the piano). To be sure, you need them in Beethoven; there are none in Bach's key-board; and Chopin does without them, to good advantage. There are *forti* and *piani;* which is not the same thing. Most disagreeable.

FRAGMENTS FROM JOURNAL

February 8, 1934.

. . . There are others, and in great number, who play and will play Bach as well and even much better than I. Not much cleverness needed for that. As for Chopin, that's another matter; a particular understanding was necessary which, as I see it, a musician who is not above all an artist can not have. I know very well what I mean by that. There is also a certain sense of the fantastic through which he is akin to Baudelaire. That kind of necessity, of logical necessitation, which henceforth had to be sought elsewhere than in counterpoint, and which, as a result, became psychological . . . As inspired, but more meditative, than Mozart.

They don't know how to play him. They falsify the very intonation of his voice. They plunge into a poem of Chopin like people who are perfectly sure in advance of what they are about. What is needed is doubt, surprise, trembling; above all, not wit ("wit makes me sick"), but not folly either; in other words: no infatuation. This is too much to ask of the virtuoso. Isn't he the one who reaps the laurels and steps in front of the artist? The creator may very well be proud (though the greatest are modest); the virtuoso is conceited. But why start that again?

April 10, 1938.

That morning I was in E major. All my thoughts involved four sharps; plus all the accidentals to happen in the course of modulation. I was transposing into E all the airs that were plaguing me with obsessive obstinacy. Besides, they weren't all vulgar and at times some phrase of the *Pastoral Symphony* or of a Bach *Largo* prevailed over *The Lads in the Navy* or the old *Song of the Cripple* of the late Paulus. All I could manage to do was replace one by the other; never to stop the current, to impose silence. Once the tune started, it continued its inexhaustible flow for hours, persisting through conversations, events, land-scapes, and probably even through my sleep, as far as I can judge by the re-sumption, as soon as I awoke, of the ob-session on which, with which, I had fallen asleep the night before. At times,

beyond all patience, I tried to interrupt
it by reciting mentally a series of verses;
but then, below my recitation, it continued as a subterranean infiltration and
it then rose up again, as, after the dis-
appearance of the Rhône, the water of
the river is seen reappearing farther off.
Some of these obsessions involved quite
a great number of measures and invited
to modulation, which enabled them to
be taken up in another key. The obses-
sion stopped only when it had run up
the scale chromatically and rejoined the
initial key. I experienced in the course
of this revolution a kind of relief on
leaving the region of the sharps to enter
that of the flats; and vice-versa, for you
can be quite sure that I had no prefer-
ence; whatever the tonality, I felt myself captive and in spite of myself un-
rolled the melody the way the squirrel
turns his cage.

I dream of a silent paradise . . .

I had reached the point of playing that *Nocturne* very well; one of those which lend themselves most to misinterpretation. It is not, moreover, one of my favorites . . . When I dream of the farewell I bade to music,

A peu que le cueur ne me fend
(My heart is nigh to breaking)

and it does not seem that there is anything death can now take from me to which I will cling more stubbornly.

January 7, 1939.

Are you thinking of stressing (but have you noticed?) the weak repeated beats of the third at the top of the accompaniment in the *Nocturne* in **D** flat (op. 27)?

Have you noticed that they fall exactly on the same off-beats as the double beats of the dominant in the slow part (in the major), likewise so extraordinarily nocturnal and so ecstatically beautiful, of the *Scherzo* in B minor? Make it be like that crystal drop which the tree-frog (or perhaps the toad) drops into the heart

94

of the purest summer nights. Was Chopin himself aware of this? . . . In any case, Paderewski was when he played the combination. In this crystalline note, both detached from all the rest and melting into it, is suspended the whole landscape.

And in both works, in similar fashion, as if stirred ecstatically, it finally rises up (in the *Nocturne* by a half-tone, in the Scherzo by a whole tone), to fall soon afterward, swooning with excess of joy.

FRAGMENTS FROM JOURNAL

January 8, 1939.

Most of these musical poems of Chopin (I am thinking, at the moment, of the *Nocturnes*) do not offer so many difficulties of execution (I mean those which the virtuoso triumphs over easily) as others of a quite different, superior order, which it seems at times that the virtuosi are not even aware of, for they pass them by and consider themselves satisfied if they perform the composition with that sovereign, imperturbable agility which almost all of them have and which leave us astounded and indifferent. As for the secret of this poem, as for the mystery, the artistic problem which governs the composition and the very genesis of the work, it seems that they have not perceived it; at all events, they in no way make us perceive it.

I believe that the first mistake is due

to the fact that they (the virtuosi) try above all to stress Chopin's romanticism, whereas what seems to me most admirable in his work is the reduction to classicism of the undeniably romantic material. This material, then the masterly subjection, is, I think, nowhere more remarkable than in the great *Nocturne* in C minor (op. 48). Nothing simpler than the composition, the proposition, of this splendid work; but still the performer must understand them himself; his playing must stress them and, in a way, *explain* them. Surprising as the sudden irruption of the wind-blasts in the second part of the work, in the major, may seem—at first so calm, so ample and solemn—astonishment must quickly yield to understanding, to the admission of the triple rhythm of the lower part, whose racing beats, when the minor comes in, must be given with perfect regularity, *reconquered,* a triumph of

97

the spiritual element over the elements unleashed at the beginning. All is lost (that is, one no longer understands anything) if it is the romanticism which triumphs. And above all: no *brio!* But what the virtuoso usually offers us is: a voice lost in the storm. This is not what Chopin was after.

How delightful, at that charming

luncheon at the home of the Paul Va-
lérys, to know that Nadia Boulanger was
in perfect agreement with me regarding
the playing of the *Preludes* and what I
had written about them (quite inade-
quately, alas!) in my *Notes on Chopin*.

UNPUBLISHED PAGES AND MISCELLANEA

SEVERAL facts, says Monsieur Ganche, give reason to believe that Frédéric Chopin had some French blood. Nicolas Chopin, Frédéric's father, was born in Lorraine, in Nancy, on August 17, 1770, and went to Warsaw around 1787. He taught the French language and always used it in his correspondence with his son, whereas Frédéric's mother and sisters wrote to him in Polish. Chopin's friends and all his contemporaries declared that he was born of a French father and he made no protest. He was aware, nevertheless,

that people might persist in this assertion for in 1835 Marie Wodzinska said
to him in a letter:

"It is our constant regret that your
name is not Chopinski, or that there are
not some other signs that you are Polish,
for in that way the French would be un-
able to dispute our glory in being your
compatriots." (Pp. 18 and 19.)

"Immediately after his death, people
began investigating the origin of his ancestors. An article published in the
Journal de Rouen of December 1, 1849
spoke of him as being descended from
the French family Chopin d'Arnouville,
one of whose members was said to have
escaped to Poland in 1685, following the
revocation of the Edict of Nantes."

Monsieur Ganche here points out
that the hypothesis is hardly likely, since
the Chopin family was Catholic.

"According to the thesis of the Poles,"
he continues, "an ancestor of Chopin

left Poland at the time Stanislas Leczin-
ski went to Lorraine." (P. 19)

A note in this work refers us to a study
by Monsieur André Lévy which appeared in the *Mercure de France* of November 16, 1912, and which, unfortu-
nately, though weakening the Polish
thesis, did not manage to oppose it with
any document. All the research done by
Monsieur Lévy and Monsieur Ganche
remains fruitless. But the absence of offi-
cial statements affirming the existence
of French ancestors of Chopin in Lorraine proves nothing, and the uncertainty continues.

At all events, it continues only regarding the question of origin, but the fact
is quite established that Chopin is one
more example of deracination, and,
moreover, of expatriation and almost
certainly of the crossing of races.

I say *one more example,* which may
confirm the truth which I consider es-

tablished, that almost all the great spirits
we glorify today, almost all the creators,
almost all those who have raised themselves above the mass, are products of
cross-breeding or, at the very least, of deracination—"seals," as Monsieur Maur-
ras once humorously called them. It
even seems to me here that after having
raised this problem regarding Chopin,
Monsieur Ganche drops it perhaps
somewhat quickly.

"Only the laws of heredity could lend
importance to the study of Chopin's an-
cestry, if his mind and work were not so
representative of the absolute character
of the Polish race. Chopin was Polish
to an extreme and he would have re-
garded a doubt about this matter as a
grave injury." (P. 20) And a little further on: "Chopin's genius is eminently
national, but, despite the uncertainty of
his French affinities, it can be claimed
that France was his second country, for

106

he found there elements which contrib-
uted to his glory."

No, this does not satisfy me; for
though I may recognize an inspiration,
an energy, that are Polish, I take a certain satisfaction in recognizing likewise
in this raw material a cut and fashion
which are French. Am I going too far?
Let us suppose that there is nothing
characteristically French in the composition of his poems, but that rather con-
tinual association with the French spirit,
with French culture, led him to exaggerate the very qualities of the Slavic
genius that were most anti-Germanic. It
is enough for me that these qualities are
essentially anti-Germanic.

Germany is the cradle of music. It is
admitted and recognized, that the German people, so inartistic and heavy, is a
musical people. Music gushes forth in
Germany in an artesian and continuous
way. It spreads all over Germany in

thick sheets. I am astonished, nonetheless, to what point certain German gen-
iuses have had to stand aloof from Germany and, I was about to say, oppose it,
in order to give shape to the monstrous
tide.

I am thinking of the Italian Mozart,
the French Gluck, the English Handel,
and leave to those more competent than
I the task of determining whether, in the
music of Bach or of the Flemish-Aus-
trian Beethoven, in short, of all of them,
what we most admire, and by means of
which this German matter really takes
shape, is not precisely the quality where-
in it is most aloof from the genius of the
race; whereas, on the other hand, the
quality by means of which it plunges
into it, that quasi-Asiatic superabund-
ance, that density, that formlessness, is
not the very element by means of which
it remains least disengaged from the barbaric, by means of which the whole of

108

Wagner's work yesterday, the budding work of a Strauss today, could exasperate the Slavic and francophile Nietzsche to the point of madness.

I have already written it elsewhere; but it can not be repeated often enough: the great instrument of culture is drawing, not music. In the former, emotion itself becomes a vassal of thought, which music, however, disperses.

The French people is a people of draughtsmen. Of artisans, stylists, draughtsmen.

Even French music is drawn.

German music accepts limits and contours only, so it seems, contrary to the genius of the race.

The piano prevails over the orchestra

as does the individual over the mass.

The unity of the ensemble can be obtained only through the depersonalization of each member.

Well-tempered clavichord; well-tempered piano. That should be taken to mean that it does not try to give itself out as something other than what it is.

Too often the piano of Beethoven imitates the orchestra, the way some pianists imitate the violin and the violin imitates the voice. The day a virtuoso gets the sound of the flute from the piano, a certain public will acclaim him. The mistake of the Goncourts, of Gautier, was their desire to throw language into the domain of painting; as that of the music of certain of today's composers is to attempt to describe, or to evoke. The perfect art is the one which first becomes aware of its limits; the former alone is limitless.

110

Play Beethoven, even Schumann, on an old tinny piano, something will always remain. Play Chopin only on an excellent piano. For the very reason that he never brings anything superfluous, he needs everything in order to be adequate. He becomes himself only when perfect. I think of him in connection with that sentence of Joubert: "For want of one virtue, the most . . . (?) soul is merely like a broken pearl."

Some of Chopin's shortest works have the necessary and pure beauty of the resolution of a problem. In art, to state a problem well is to solve it.

A short poem or musical composition was very rarely composed in the order in which we read it. Probably it sometimes happens that the opening measures, the first lines, were invented last. In the presence of a sonnet by Baudelaire or a prelude by Chopin I like to wonder what the initial idea was, what was the material that first presented itself to the composer's mind, around which all the rest slowly formed and coordinated. This quest may seem rather vain, for the work of art is fully realized only if this genesis can no longer be recognized in it. And I think that often the artist himself ceases to be conscious of it at the moment of inspiration. But the labor of composition, for a musical poem of Chopin, is by no means the same as that of a Bach fugue. Here the theme is necessarily initial, and can probably be slightly modified according to the necessities of the counterpoint, but is nevertheless always the original material.

112

How simple Chopin's musical propositions are . . .

One of the loveliest nocturnes, in C sharp minor, first shows quite simply the minor third becoming, upon reaching the higher half-tone, a leading tone, whereas the subsiding tonic becomes a sub-dominant of the related key into which one enters. And what it takes me several words to express is as simple as a problem for children.

The introductory phrase of the first ballade is only a seventh chord whose

whole stress is on the retardation, by a kind of appoggiatura, of the last note

113

which immediately falls back into the tonic; and this makes a perfect gesture of extraordinary incantatory power.

Yes, Chopin, and this is important to note, allows himself to be led and advised by the notes . . .

And if, among his *Etudes,* I consider the one which breathes a feeling of utter desolation (B flat minor), I admire a triumphant and splendid serenity which he achieves by degrees, through successive modulations where the anguished soul seems finally to escape its agitation. But, even here, I hold that it is not so much the feeling, which dictates the modulation and chord, but rather the exact sense of a musical propriety in which the feeling comes to dwell quite naturally, (as it does in a verse of Valéry, for example, which only the propriety of the rhyme, of the rhythm, of the choice of words, of the syntax suggests and prescribes and submits to his perfect taste).

114

I give up trying to find out the advantage the virtuosi find in playing *presto* the shower of eighth notes which, at regular intervals, interrupt the grave and mysterious chorale of the middle of the third scherzo. This passage should be played in the exact rhythm of the tempo adopted for the chorale, beginning on the second beat just as it is scored; not slowly and as if released suddenly by a spring. It is a warm and gentle rain, in which a rainbow may be smiling. Played without haste.

Precisely in order to maintain amidst these eighths the tempo of the chorale, it is well not to take the latter in too slow a movement. There is nothing

more abominable than the practice of slowing up the *lento* the more so as the performer proposes to speed up the *vivace*—out of a kind of compensation—or rather out of a quest for an effect which has nothing in common with art. In the passage in question, the pianist who plays the run in eighths too quickly is the very one who plays the chorale too slowly—for effect. No change of speed from one to the other is admissible. People like that are lunatics.

Prelude in G flat major.
Is there in all music a more enveloping, a more tender gesture? Each decisive note is achieved only when it has first been circumvented, by an exquisite approach which makes it hope and which lets it wait. I like these first measures of discovery to be somewhat hesitant, as of one who dares not dare, then abandons himself to that charming effusion in which superabundant joy blends with melancholy; then everything melts under the caress in an amorous abandon.

I really must confess that I have small taste for certain of Chopin's great and most famous compositions—the *Allegro de concert,* the *Polonaise-Fantaisie* (op. 61) and even the great and so highly cried up *Fantaisie* in F minor. These are show-pieces for the great public, declamatory and somewhat redundant, hence of a facile pathos, for effect, where I just barely find the incomparable artist of the *Preludes* and the *Etudes.* I never have any desire to play them, and still less to hear them. I leave them to the professionals who obtain easy successes with them in drawing-rooms. I shall therefore be excused for saying nothing about them.

On the other hand, the *Barcarolle* and the *Berceuse* which often stray into this collection of "concert pieces" are two of my favorites and I am more than half inclined to put the *Barcarolle,* as did Nietzsche, at the pinnacle of Chopin's work.

I shall speak about it at some length later on. But I should like to point out before, in passing, that these two works are steeped in an extraordinary joy; the *Berceuse* in a tender and quite feminine joy; the *Barcarolle* in a kind of radiant, graceful and robust lyricism which explains Nietzsche's predilection . . . and mine.

LETTER FROM M. ED. GANCHE TO ANDRÉ GIDE CONCERNING THE NOTES ON CHOPIN

LETTER FROM M. ED. GANCHE

It seems to me interesting, even indispensable, to print in its entirety a letter I received from M. Edouard Ganche regarding my *Notes on Chopin*.

January 2, 1932.

Dear Sir,

It probably does not much matter to you that someone reports the extreme satisfaction he derived from your Notes on Chopin. *It is the work of a master in the art of music. You will be more pleased, perhaps, to receive answers to your questions, and, assuming this to be so, I take the liberty of giving them to you.*

The First Prelude *is scored by Chopin:* Agitato.

Nocturne in G minor. *I must say that the organ points are Chopin's, and this one time, if I may say so, it is not possible to incriminate the revisers.*

In the second **Prelude,** *nothing odd. It is the exact notation of a knell tolled by two bells in the belfry of a village church. Whether because the bells did not harmonize or because the sound was modified by the action of the wind, or for both these reasons, I always heard, in my childhood, this mournful knell, just as dissonant, announcing a death and approaching burial, just as Chopin reproduced it with the same funereal dissonances and as he certainly must have heard it in the solitude of Polish villages.*

Prelude in D minor, *No. 24. In Chopin the quarter note ceases to be marked in the lower part from the* **ninth** *measure on. There are no staccato or legato notes.*

I own the original French edition of Chopin's complete works corrected by him. This is a unique collection for which we are indebted to his pupil Jane Stirling. I cite among a hundred details unknown today, because Chopin's revisers and pupils—Mikuli, to cite only one—found that his wonderful innovations were gross faults or oversights—a few original notations.

In the 14th Prelude, *which was always marked* Allegro *even in the original edition, Chopin has completely crossed out the word* Allegro *and written above in big letters:* Largo.

Next to it: Pesante, *in Chopin's hand.*

Sonata in B minor.—*Largo 27th and 28th measures:*

Although the A is sharp in the clef, Chopin has pencilled in, before the A, a

very heavily drawn sharp in order to show that it is really intended.—(Unresolved appoggiatura, very bold. Even today one must get used to it.—They are often found in Chopin, but the revisers have deleted everything. They have cried out, the imbeciles, that Chopin's manuscripts were full of mistakes.)

I own the manuscript of the **Barcarolle,** *the first and genuine work sheet. The "sfogato" that you admire is there.*

Chopin paid no attention to symmetry and pendants. He almost always modified repeated measures; the revisers hastened to make everything uniform. Chopin's syncopations have almost everywhere been changed. These massacres made me decide to undertake the long and painful labor of the great edition of Chopin's works for the Oxford University Press.